The message of this first story is to remember not to take good people for granted.

Treat everyone with kindness and treat them in the best way just how you would like to be treated.

Dedicated to all children, you are our future!

—more stories to follow.

Darren St Mart

Once upon a time, a Lowly Chicken lived with a Bee colony. How this Lowly Chicken wished for an animal friend.

His adopted Mother was the Queen Bee of the large bee colony.
Even though he was a chicken, she and the worker bees did not mind him because they all loved him.

Until one day, the Lowly Chicken declared, "I am a chicken, and I want an animal friend!"

Well, the Queen Bee got into a terrible state. She didn't know what to do. "Oh, dear," she said to her herself. "He's a chicken. All I know are bees, not other animals really!"

You see, the Queen found the Lowly Chicken abandoned when he was just a little chick.

One day, when he and his family were out shopping. A great big alligator came up from behind and began to gobble them all up! The Lowly Chicken did not know what to do because he was busy walking in front and not looking back.

Gulp...gulp...gulp...one by one, they all got gobbled up, disappearing into the alligator's mouth, until it came to the Lowly Chicken's turn. He was in a terrible state.

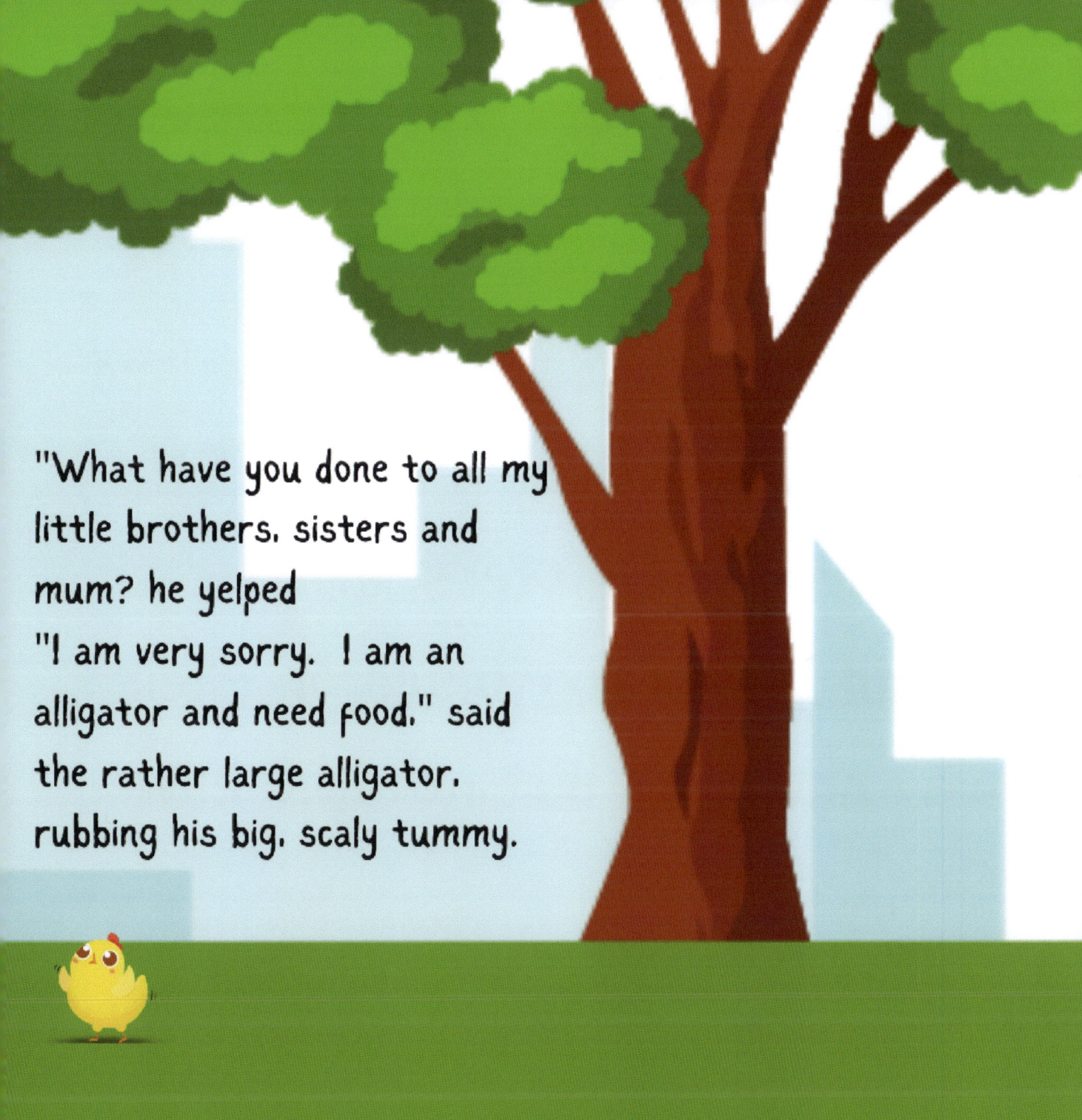

"What have you done to all my little brothers, sisters and mum? he yelped
"I am very sorry. I am an alligator and need food." said the rather large alligator, rubbing his big, scaly tummy.

The alligator took pity on the Lowly Chicken, so he opened his mouth very wide and out walked the Lowly Chicken's mum, little brothers and sisters, all safe and sound. They continued on their way shopping, but not the Lowly Chicken.

He just stood there, shocked. "What gave you the right to eat all my little brothers, sisters and mum?" he flapped, feeling rather brave because he had now met an understanding alligator."

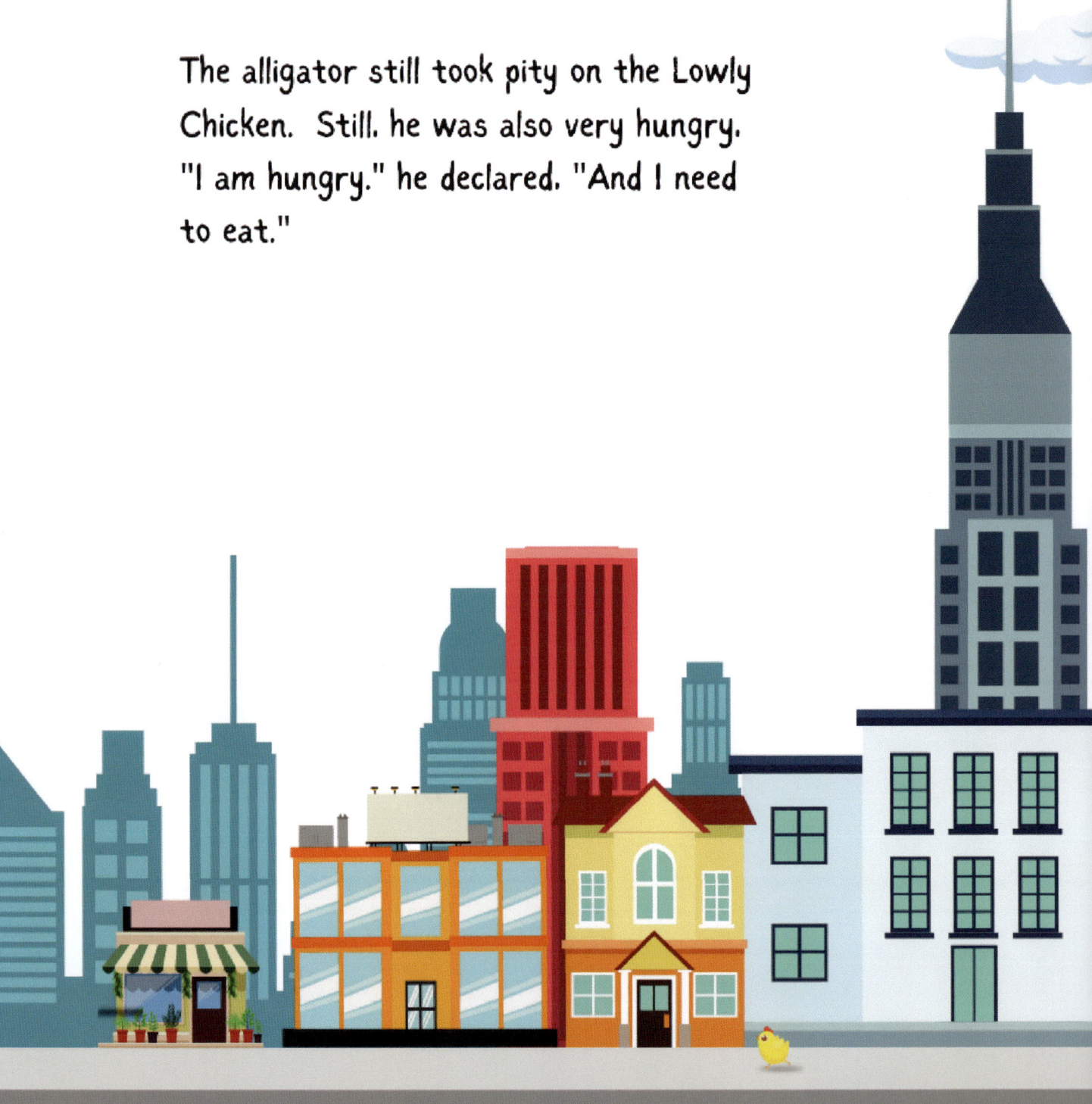

The alligator still took pity on the Lowly Chicken. Still. he was also very hungry. "I am hungry." he declared. "And I need to eat."

Then, licking his lips, he began to chase the Lowly Chicken down the street and around the shops. "Here, chicky...chicky...chicky!" he called out as he chased the Lowly Chicken from shop to shop and from street to street.

At that very moment, the Queen Bee was flying overhead with her squadron of worker bees behind her. Looking down, she, too, like the alligator, took pity on the Lowly Chicken being chased by the now-hungry alligator. So, swooping down, leading her squadron, she ordered them to pick up the Lowly Chicken and whisked him off to her beehive. They all did this with excellent efficiency, by the way.

"Phew!" gasped the Queen Bee, looking on leading ahead at her worker bees carrying the Lowly Chicken as they rose up into the air to escape the jaws of the hungry alligator. "You are very heavy!"

The alligator stopped chasing to watch what he thought was his next meal flying off into the distance. So he decided to lie down and take a nap after all that running.

Whilst airborne, the Queen Bee asked caringly, "Are you hungry?" as she led the working bees back to her hive. "I am a chicken, we're always hungry," declared the Lowly Chicken, looking down at the countryside rolling by.

"Yes, I can see that," replied the Queen Bee, somewhat amused that just a few moments ago, he was being chased around town by a ravenous alligator intent on gobbling him up and now, being saved by her and her worker bees.

They started to descend. and the Lowly Chicken could see in the distance the bee hive ahead. Worker bees from the hive started to fly up to greet them as they began their approach to land.

"Your Highness," asked one politely to the Queen. "Would the gentleman like a cup of honey tea?"

"Honey Tea!....DELICIOUS!...." called out another worker bee, checking on the Lowly Chicken, carrying squadron, as they all touched down with a gentle thump.

The Queen bee, looking amused, gave permission with a regal wave, saying," Of course, an excellent idea."

Well, the Lowly Chicken did not hesitate. He grabbed the mug of honey tea from the approaching worker bee and gulped it down without even saying thank you!

After a while, the Lowly Chicken became tired and, with a loud, lazy yawn, announced, "I want to go to sleep."

The Queen Bee again felt sorry for the Lowly Chicken. "You can sleep in a bed of honey we made specially for you."

And with that, the Lowly Chicken stuck his beak up in the air and flopped straight into bed.

The following morning, the Lowly Chicken got up to a lovely pot of porridge and tea, all made of honey.

For years, the Queen and the worker bees all loved the Lowly Chicken, but he would have none of it. Always offering him love, but he would simply point to his tummy. "I'm hungry," he would always say.

Well, today, he wanted to have an animal friend. The Queen Bee was in a terrible state. She ordered all the worker bees to go and visit as many farms as possible. None of the farmyard animals wanted to know the lowly chicken, so instead, by order of the Queen they collected as many farm eggs as possible in exchange for their delicious honey. For she knew deep down that other farmyard animals knew of the Lowly Chicken's ungrateful behaviour, but she had to try.

Buzz...buzz...buzz...they said as they went about their business, visiting farms and politely asking if they could have some eggs in exchange for their delicious honey.

Not one worker bee protested, each doing as they were told because, like the Queen bee, they all loved him.

The grand day came when so many eggs were collected. The Queen bee ordered a public holiday. "We will have a public holiday," she declared. "Hooray!" all the worker bees cheered. With the sound of trumpets, the Queen bee proudly presented all the collected eggs to the Lowly Chicken. Hoping that it would cheer him up, as alas, they could not find any animal friends for him.

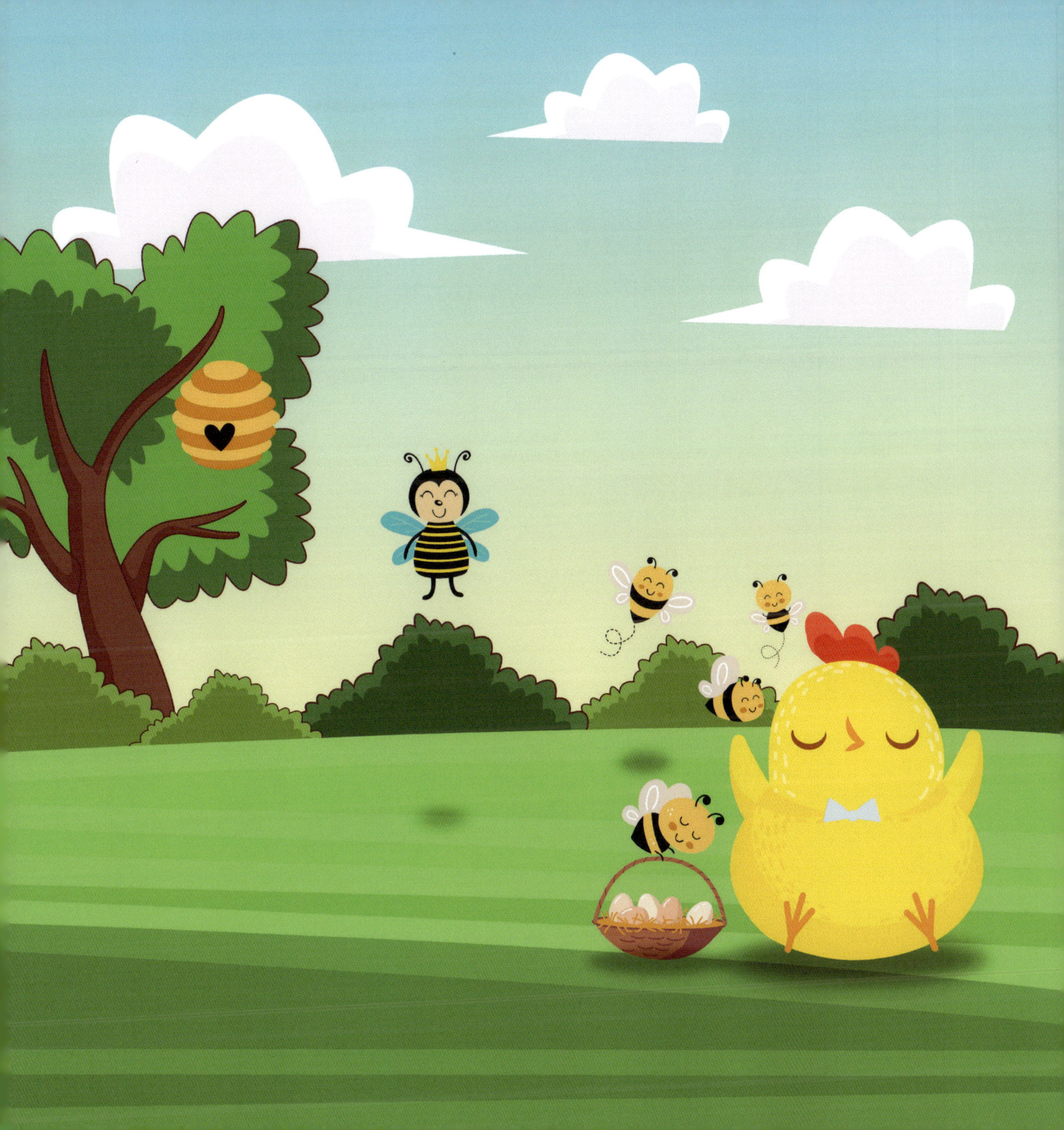

The Lowly Chicken stood there, realising that this was not what he wanted. Instead of saying thank you so much, your Royal Highness and worker bees, for trying. He angrily picked up each egg and threw them all up in the air with a mischievous grin.
At that very moment, a flock of geese, a squadron, was flying south for the winter.

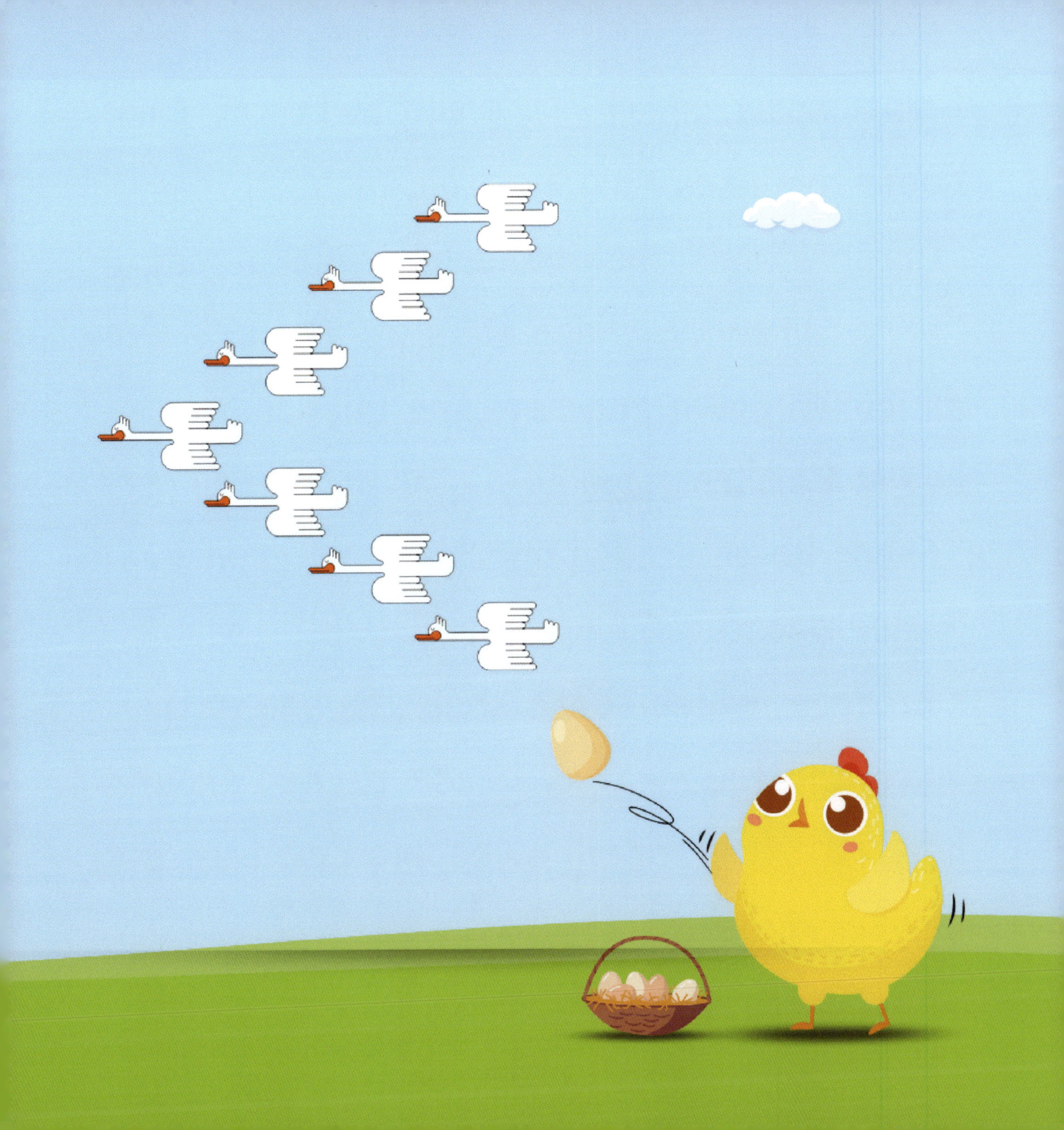

Splat...splat...splat...each egg battered each goose like great big custard pies. "Brrrrr!" said the squadron leader goose. "Who threw all those eggs up at us?" They all looked down and saw the misbehaving Lowly Chicken flapping his wings in delight. "There he is!" called out the squadron leader goose. "COME ON, DIVE!" the squadron leader goose shouted, and with that, the squadron of geese turned around, heading back, and all swooping down at the Lowly Chicken.

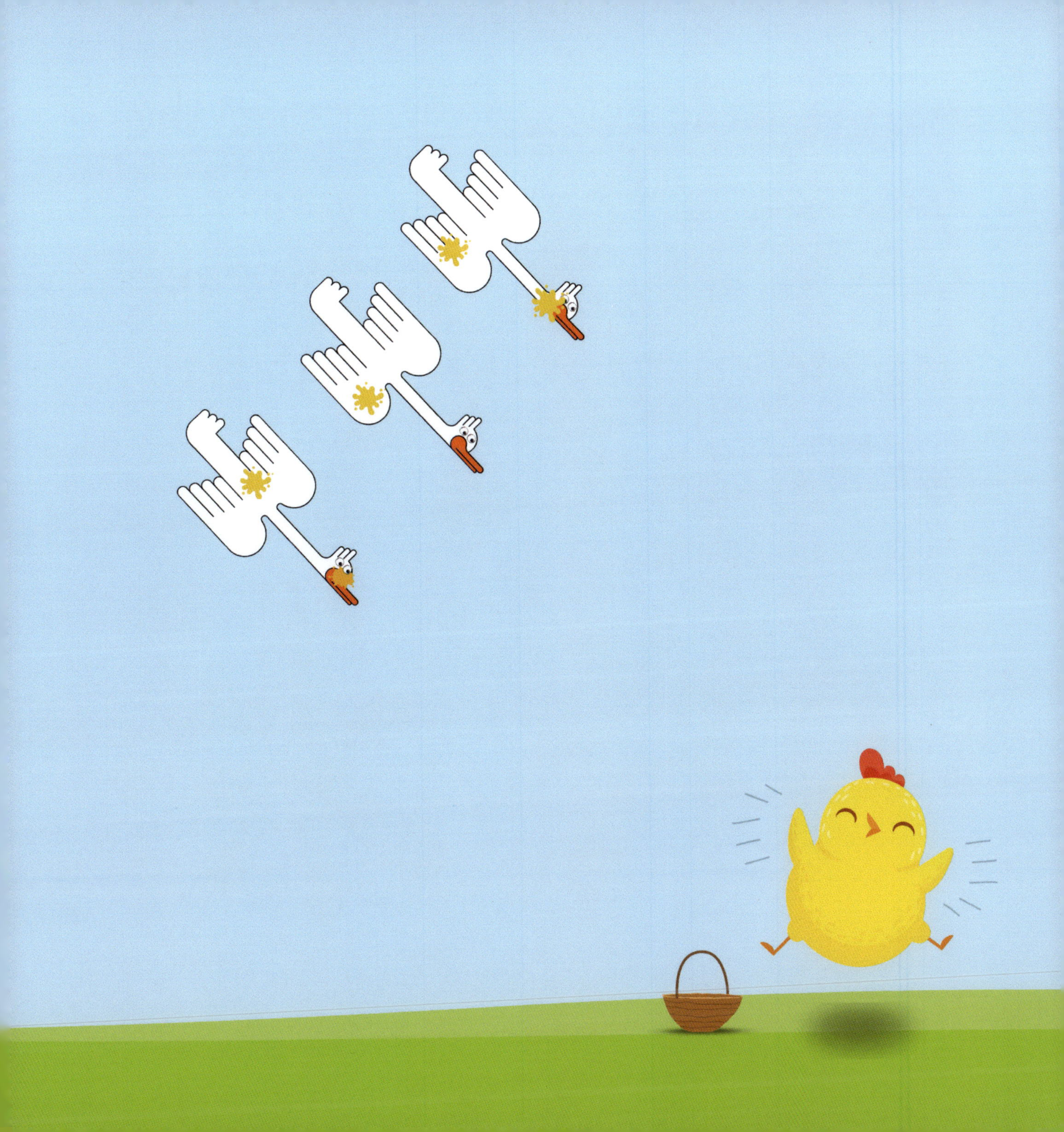

As the geese dove, they scraped the remainder of the eggs from their faces, throwing them back onto the ungrateful Lowly Chicken with big splats.

The Queen and worker bees all took off for safety, but not the Lowly Chicken. For you see, chickens can't fly but can only run, so run he did until he reached town.

In town, everyone ignored him. They knew he was the Lowly Chicken.
Every time he asked for food, they would give him chicken feed but not any love.

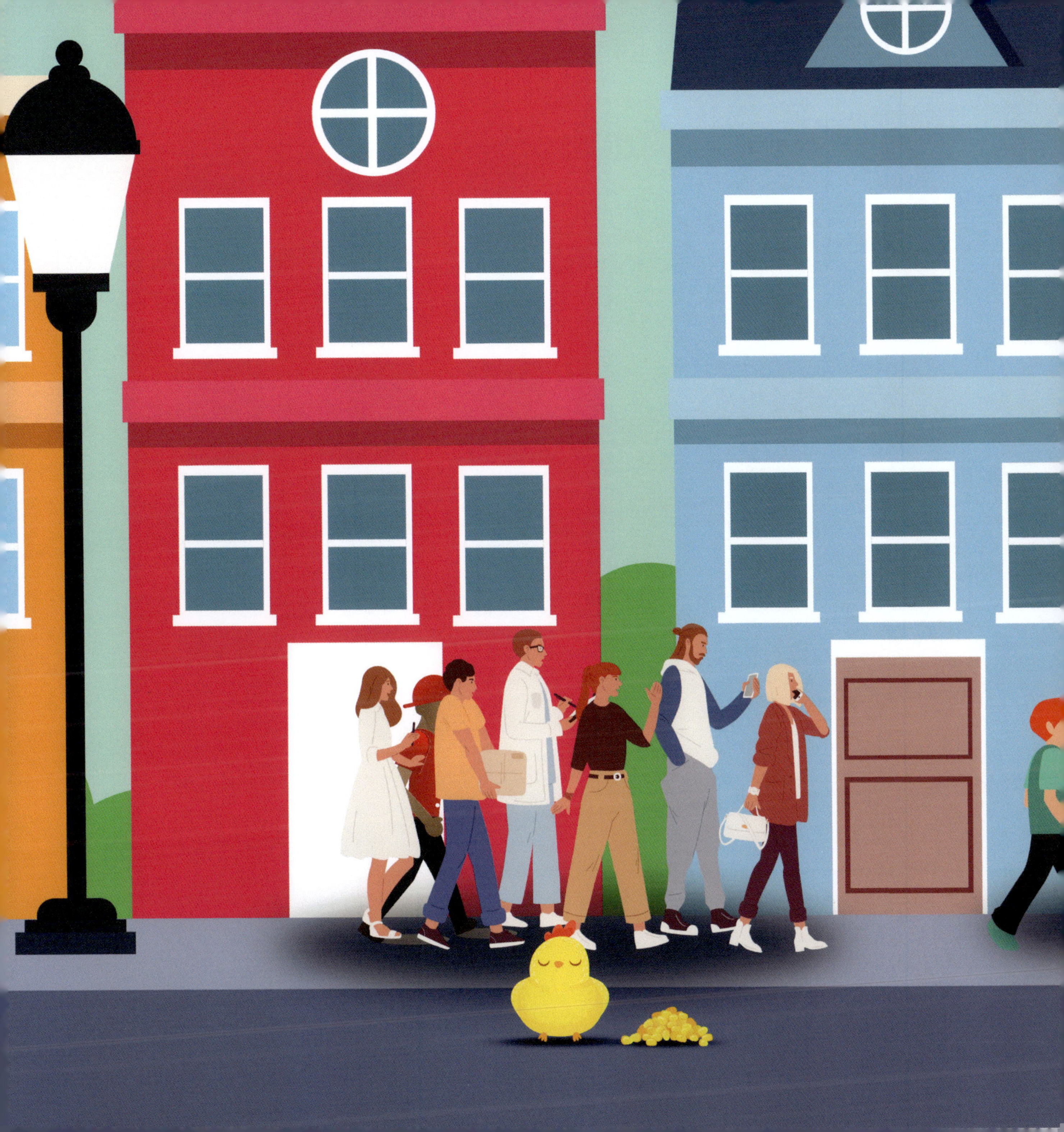

This continued until a little girl approached him one day as he sat lonely and miserable by the curbside, his head hung down in his wings.

She asked, "Why are you so sad?"

The Lowly Chicken looked up sadly and replied, "I had everything. I had a kind Mother, in the form of the Queen Bee, a loving family in the worker bees, and I didn't love them back." he began to sob. "I took them all for granted."

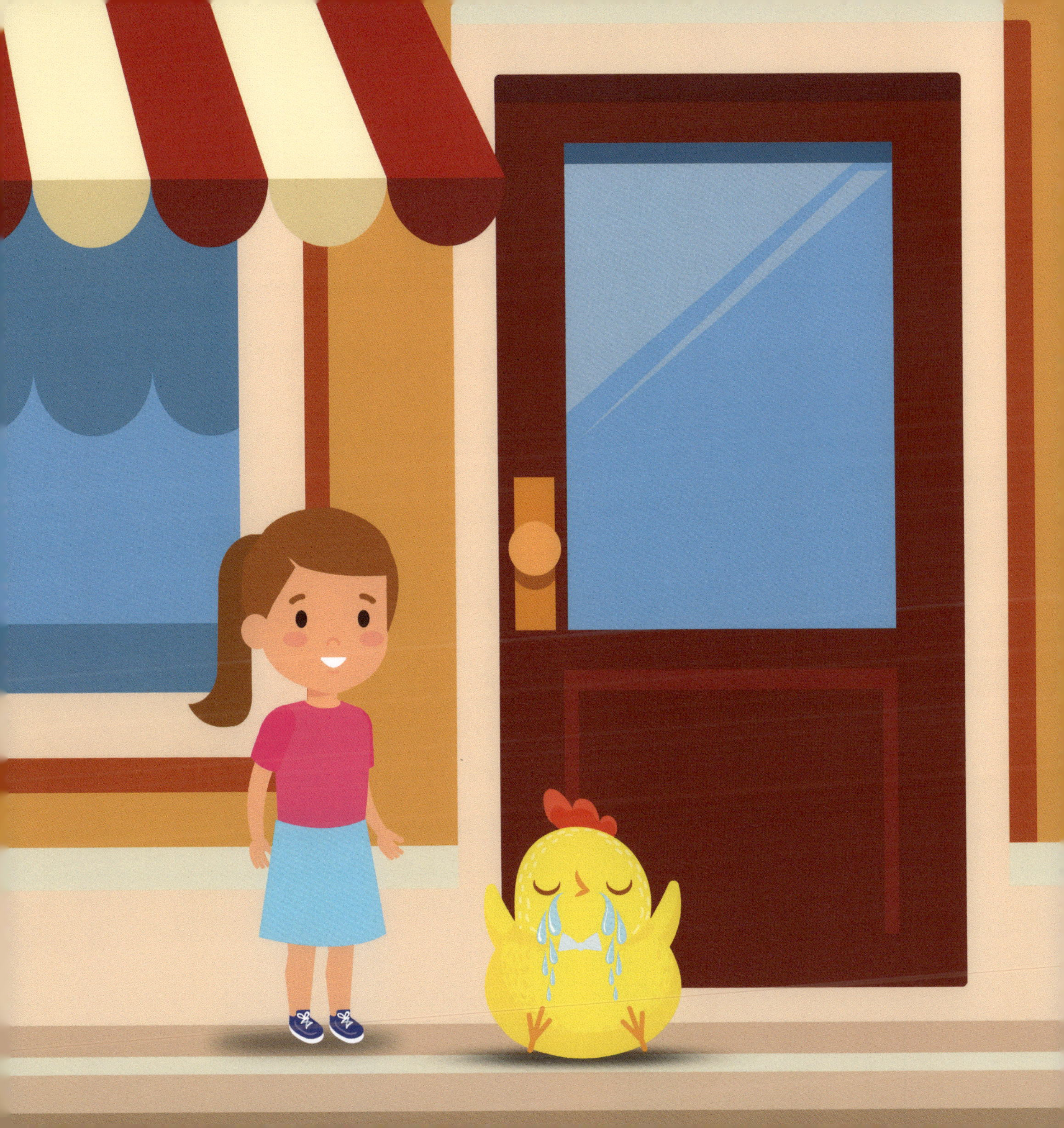

The little girl took pity on him, but before asking her Mother, who was coming out of the shops holding something, if they could take the Lowly Chicken home, she asked, "What have you learned?"

The Lowly Chicken looked up and replied, "I have learned to love by not taking anybody for granted who loves me."

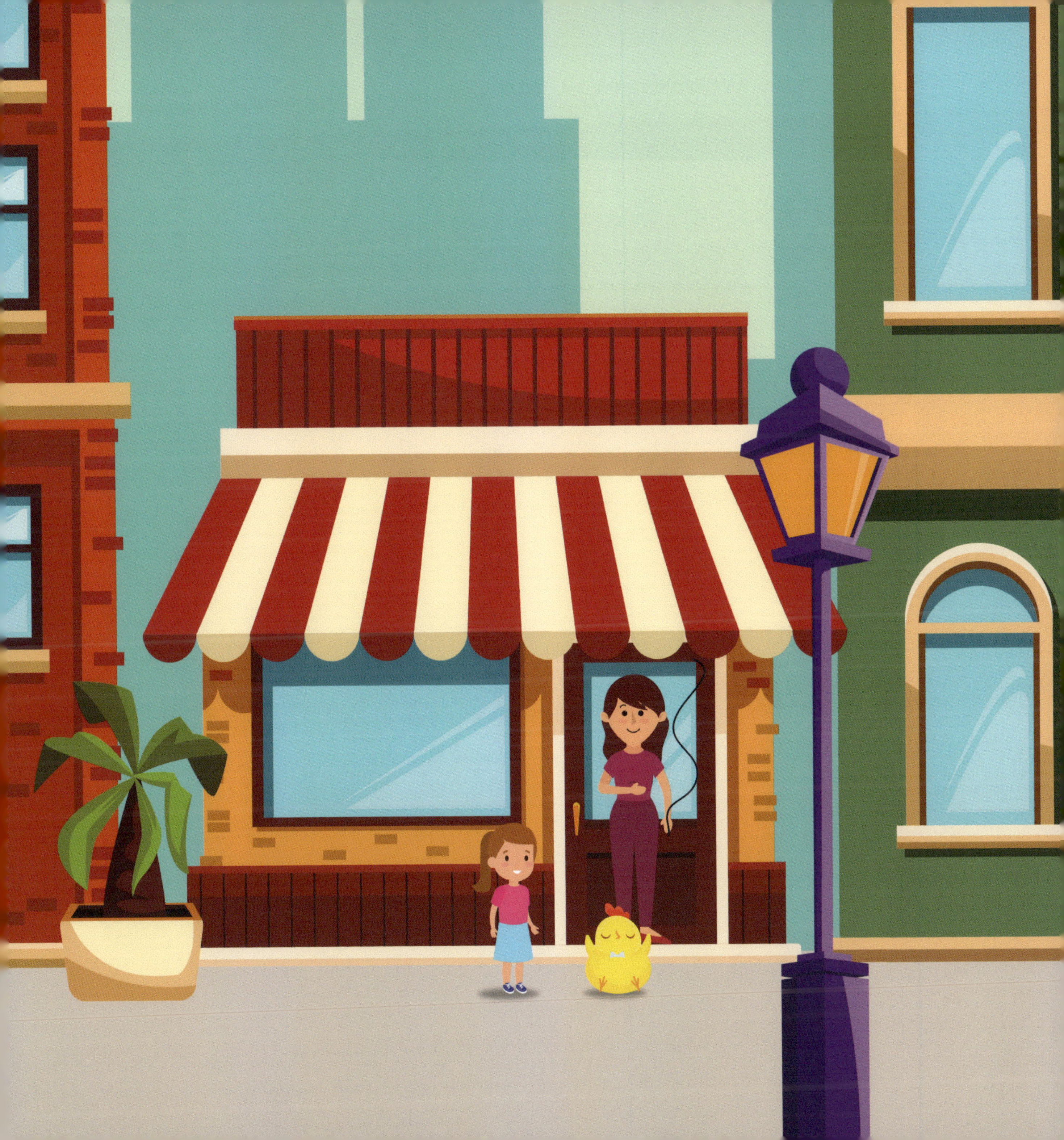

At that moment, the Mother, overhearing, walked up, holding a red balloon she had bought for her daughter. She looked lovingly at her daughter and then at the Lowly Chicken.

"Here, have this balloon as a gift. You are welcome to come home with us, which is a farm. We can give you shelter and warmth. We are a friendly bunch. I'm sure we will all get on"

Upon hearing this, the little girl jumped in the air, "Yippee!" letting out a little cheer. The Lowly Chicken graciously took the red balloon, "Thank you," he said graciously. My name is Abigail," said the little girl, "and this is my Mummy."
Then, looking up at her Mummy, she asked sweetly, "Mummy, what is your name please?"
Abigail's Mother replied, "My name is Jenny," looking at the Lowly Chicken, she asked, "And what is your name?"
The Lowly Chicken, lowering his head, quietly answered, "Everybody calls me the Lowly Chicken."

Abigail thought briefly for a moment. Then, saying, "I know, we will call you Henry."

"My name is Henry!" Henry lifted his head with a smile. "I have a proper name!"

With that, Henry got up and began following Jenny and Abigail to their farm, where he made many farmyard friends.

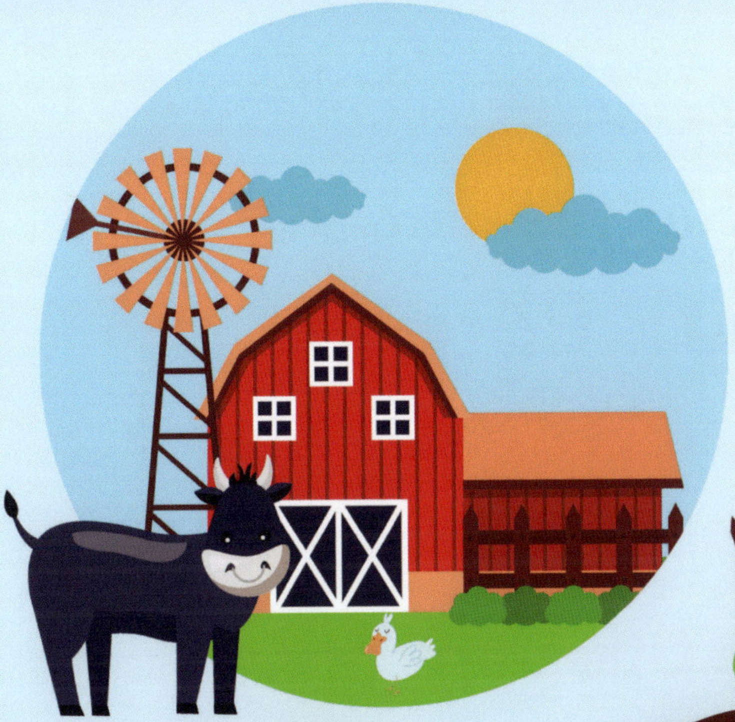
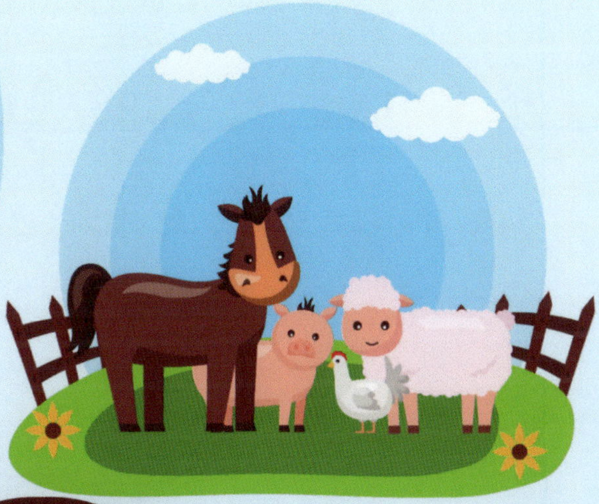
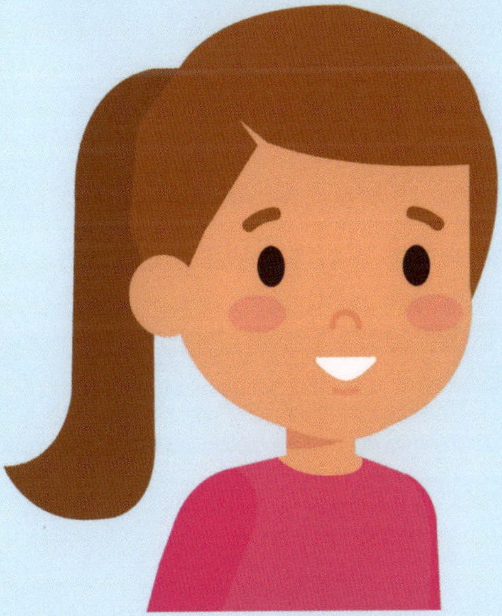
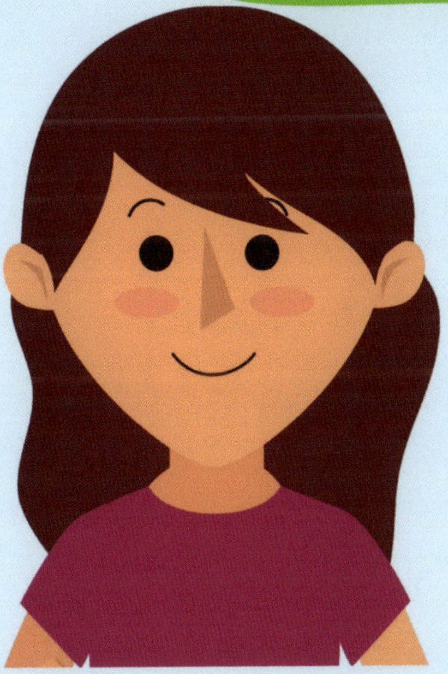
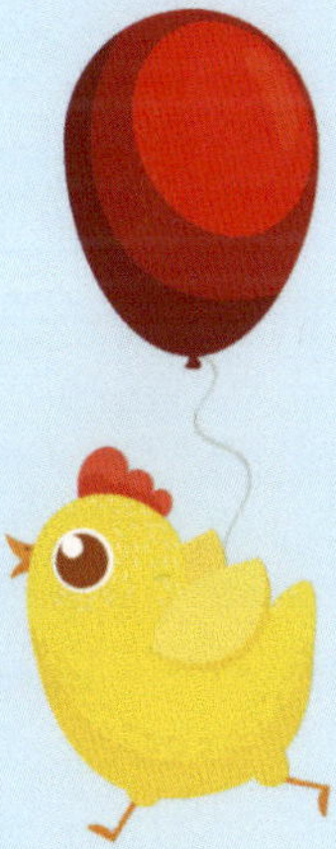

From then on, Henry never complained. He never whined. He was just thankful for what he was given. He realised then how much the Queen bee and the worker bees loved and cared for him. He loved them in his own way, but unfortunately didn't show it.

Henry learned a very valuable season which was not taking people for granted.

Henry was given a second chance in this story, so please be kind and loving to each other

THE END.

Please feel free to follow me on social media, where there are motivational videos, pictures and news for adults and children alike.

📷 thelowlychicken

f the lowly chicken and other children's stories

Dear reader(s),

Thank you so much for reading my book 'The Lowly Chicken.'

I hope you enjoyed reading it, either on your own or with someone else. Please feel free to add your comments to my Amazon page as a review of what you learned. I would love to read. Remember, I am here to encourage you to be kind to each other.

I want to thank all the kind people who have helped me with my 2nd edition. Family, friends, and YouTubers thank you for sharing your knowledge to help people like myself.
You get back what you give out - my heartfelt thanks to you all.

Lots of love,

Darren St Mart

Printed in Great Britain
by Amazon